BACKYARD JUNGLE

SAFARI

GRAY SQUIRRELS

Tammy Gagne

PURPLE TOAD
PUBLISHING

Printing   2   3   4   5   6   7   8   9

BACKYARD JUNGLE
SAFARI

Foxes
Gray Squirrels
Opossums
Raccoons

Publisher's Cataloging-in-Publication data
Gagne, Tammy
  Gray squirrel / written and illustrated by Tammy Gagne.
    p. cm.
Includes bibliographic references and index.
ISBN 9781624691041
1. Gray squirrel—Juvenile literature. 2. Squirrels—Habits and behavior. I. Series : Backyard jungle safari.
QL737 2015
  599.36

Library of Congress Control Number: 2014945186

eBook ISBN: 9781624691058

ABOUT THE AUTHOR: Tammy Gagne is a freelance writer who has authored numerous books for both adults and children. In her spare time, she enjoys visiting schools to speak to children about the writing process. She resides in northern New England with her husband, son, and a menagerie of animals—including two degus, Chilean ground squirrels..

PUBLISHER'S NOTE: The information in this book has been researched in depth, and to the best of our knowledge is correct. Although every measure is taken to give an accurate account, Purple Toad Publishing makes no warranty of the accuracy of the information and is not liable for damages caused by inaccuracies.

BACKYARD JUNGLE
SAFARI
GRAY SQUIRRELS

"Shhh!" Jack says to his little sister, Sophia. "Try not to make a single sound as we tip-toe down the steps to embark on our backyard safari." Jack knows that if they are quiet, they just might encounter the Eastern gray squirrel. If it spots them first, though, this nimble rodent will likely run away.

More than 200
kinds of squirrels
exist today.

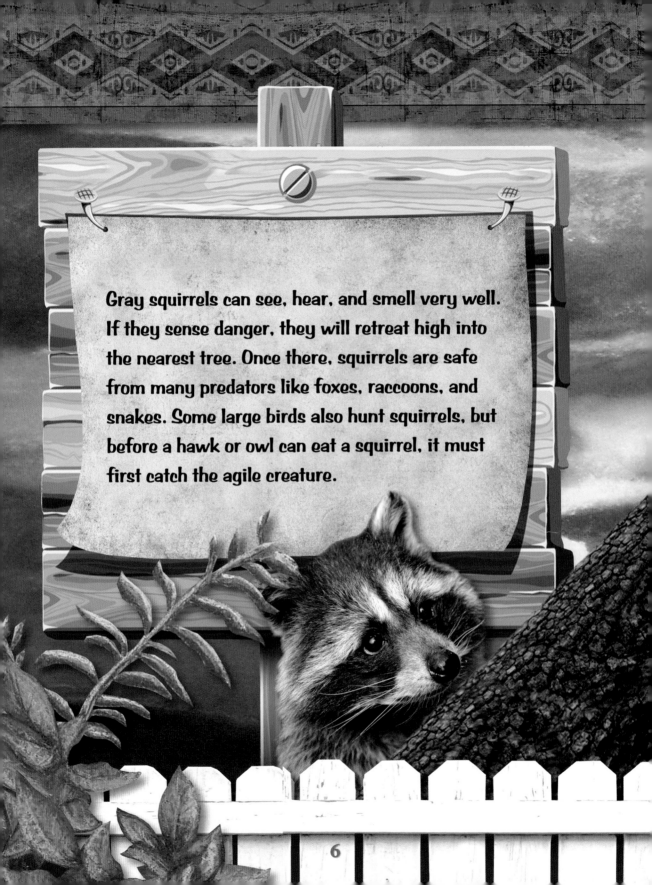

Gray squirrels can see, hear, and smell very well. If they sense danger, they will retreat high into the nearest tree. Once there, squirrels are safe from many predators like foxes, raccoons, and snakes. Some large birds also hunt squirrels, but before a hawk or owl can eat a squirrel, it must first catch the agile creature.

Squirrels can live up to 20 years! Even so, many are killed by predators like foxes long before they reach this age.

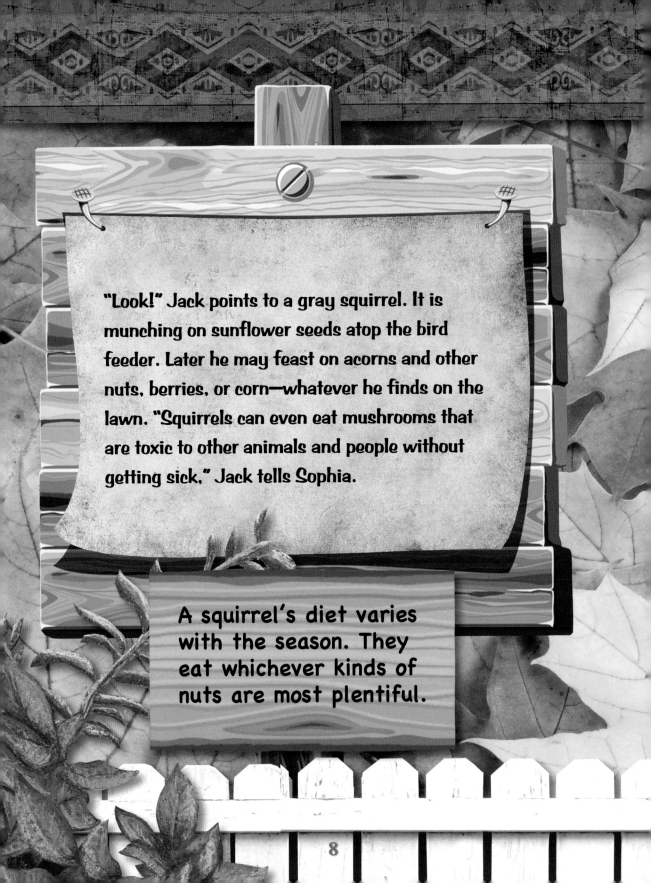

"Look!" Jack points to a gray squirrel. It is munching on sunflower seeds atop the bird feeder. Later he may feast on acorns and other nuts, berries, or corn—whatever he finds on the lawn. "Squirrels can even eat mushrooms that are toxic to other animals and people without getting sick," Jack tells Sophia.

A squirrel's diet varies with the season. They eat whichever kinds of nuts are most plentiful.

The first thing they notice about the gray squirrel is its long, bushy tail. This body part gives the animal its family name: Sciuridae (see-YUR-ih-dye) meaning "shadow-tailed." All squirrels belong to this family.

A squirrel's tail is about as long as its entire body.

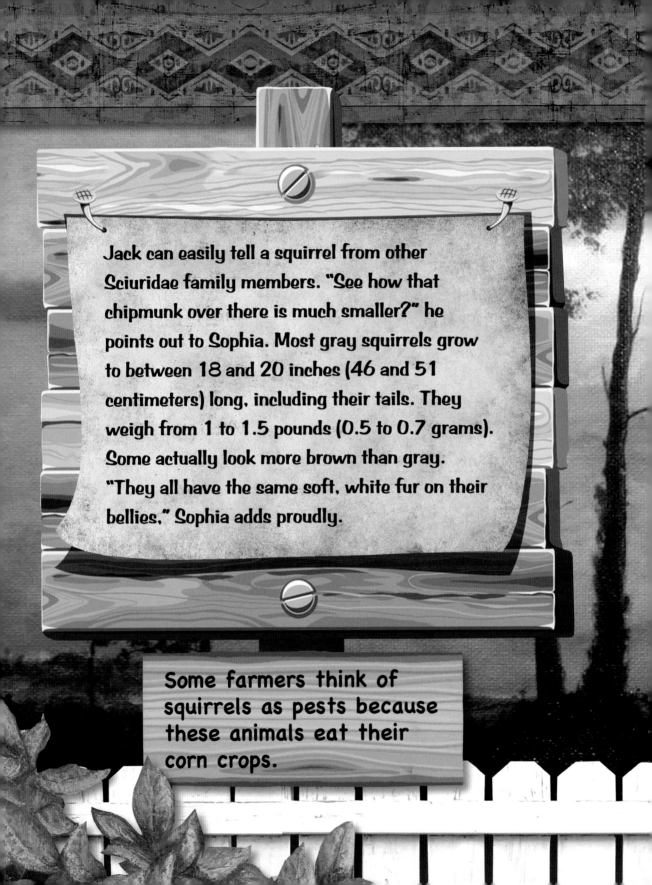

Jack can easily tell a squirrel from other Sciuridae family members. "See how that chipmunk over there is much smaller?" he points out to Sophia. Most gray squirrels grow to between 18 and 20 inches (46 and 51 centimeters) long, including their tails. They weigh from 1 to 1.5 pounds (0.5 to 0.7 grams). Some actually look more brown than gray. "They all have the same soft, white fur on their bellies," Sophia adds proudly.

Some farmers think of squirrels as pests because these animals eat their corn crops.

Large numbers of Eastern gray squirrels are found throughout the eastern half of the United States. Western gray squirrels only live in California, Oregon, and Washington. The Western grays are a threatened species. It is illegal to hunt, trap, or kill them in Washington.

Squirrels use their tails to help keep their balance on high tree branches.

Squirrels eat many of the same foods that wild birds do. They especially love sunflower seeds.

"Uh-oh!" Sophia cries. A mother blue jay is on her way to the feeder now. The squirrel knows it's time to scurry away. Gray squirrels get along with most small animals, but this particular bird noticed the gray squirrel trying to steal an egg from her nest yesterday. The high number of squirrels in the neighborhood has driven this squirrel to eating eggs.

"Tchrr, tchrr!" Just past that big oak tree, two more squirrels capture Jack and Sophia's attention. The animals are chasing one another, chattering away. The smaller one is a young female. She used to play like this with her two brothers, but hasn't seen them since they left their mother at around 12 weeks of age. Female squirrels breed each year between December and January. About 45 days later, they give birth.

A baby squirrel weighs about an ounce (28 grams) at birth.

Squirrels always have to be on the lookout. Cats can run more than twice as fast as they can.

"Oh no," Sophia frets. It looks like the playful pair has attracted some unwanted attention. A Maine Coon cat was thinking about stalking the blue jay. But the noisy squirrels have given it another idea. The squirrels escape before the cat can catch them. Nonetheless, the cat has fun making the squirrels dash away into the woods.

Soon these squirrels will have something more important than play on their minds: storing food. Adult gray squirrels spend their days foraging. They bury acorns and other goodies in scattered locations. Unfortunately, they often forget where they hide their treasures. "That is how a number of oak trees are planted," Jack shares.

A squirrel can find and bury up to 25 nuts in about an hour.

Squirrels don't hibernate the way other animals, like bears, do. Instead, they remain active all year long. They build nests of leaves and twigs high up in the trees. This is where squirrels sleep at night. They also stay in their nests to keep warm and dry during bad weather.

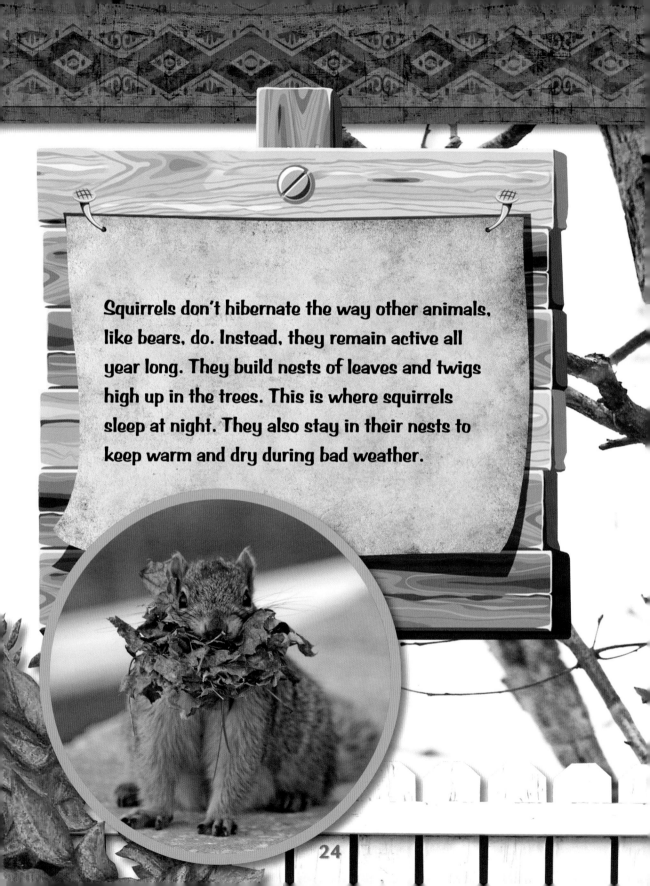

A squirrel's nest is called a drey.

When gray squirrels aren't in their nests, they can be seen in a variety of habitats. They scamper through backyards, forest floors, and city parks every day. After darting up trees, they jump from branch to branch with amazing balance. They can even jump from one tree to another.

Some squirrels have been known to leap up to 10 feet (3 meters) at a time.

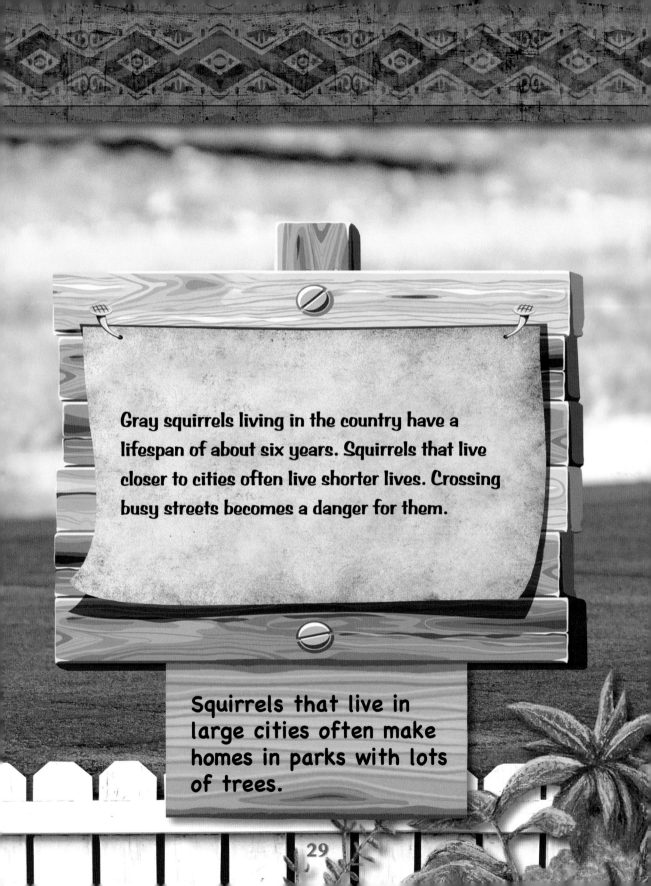

Gray squirrels living in the country have a lifespan of about six years. Squirrels that live closer to cities often live shorter lives. Crossing busy streets becomes a danger for them.

Squirrels that live in large cities often make homes in parks with lots of trees.

You are most likely to spot a pair of squirrels together in late winter or early spring.

"Aw," Sophia says as she spots the female squirrel once again. It looks like she has caught the eye of a suitor. With the blue jay gone, the bird feeder bandit has returned; however, playing with a pretty girl sounds much more fun than eating seeds alone. Chasing away his competition, the male chatters to the long-tailed lady. Off the pair go to explore the treetops together.

FURTHER READING

Further Reading
Books
Adam, Rubin. *Those Darn Squirrels!* New York: HMH Books for Young Readers, 2011.

Bommersbach, Jana. *A Squirrel's Story: A True Tale.* Chandler, AZ: Little Five Star, 2013.

Stein, David Ezra. *Ol' Mama Squirrel.* New York: Nancy Paulsen Books, 2013.

Works Consulted
Curtis, Paul D., and Kristi L. Sullivan. "Tree Squirrels." Wildlife Damage Management Fact Sheet Series, Cornell Cooperative Extension, Wildlife Damage Management Program. http://wildlifecontrol.info/pubs/Documents/Squirrels/Squirrel_factsheet.pdf.

Hamilton, Garry. *Super Species: The Creatures That Will Dominate the Planet.* Buffalo: Firefly Books, 2010.

On the Internet
Mushroom: The Journal of Wild Mushrooming http://www.mushroomthejournal.com/greatlakesdata/Terms/squir27.html#Squirrelsa

National Geographic, Squirrel http://animals.nationalgeographic.com/animals/mammals/squirrel/

The Squirrel Place http://www.squirrels.org/index.php

State of Connecticut, Department of Energy and Environmental Protection http://www.ct.gov/deep/cwp/view.asp?a=2723&q=326018

Washington Department of Fish and Wildlife, 2012 Annual Report http://wdfw.wa.gov/conservation/endangered/species/western_gray_squirrel.pdf

Wildlife Rescue League http://www.wildliferescueleague.org/pdf/squirrels.pdf

INDEX